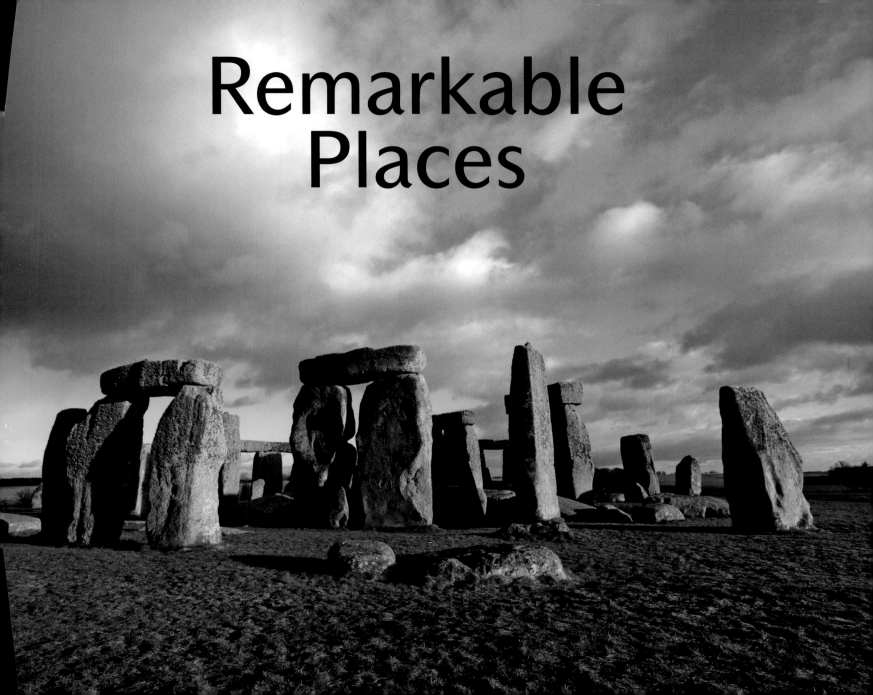

Remarkable Places

Remarkable Places

Explore the beauty of nature's hidden places

Bath · New York · Singapore · Hong Kong · Cologne · Delhi
Melbourne · Amsterdam · Johannesburg · Auckland · Shenzhen

First published by Parragon in 2010

Parragon
Queen Street House
4 Queen Street
Bath BA1 1HE, UK

Designed, produced and packaged by
Stonecastle Graphics Limited

Designed by Paul Turner and Sue Pressley
Edited by Philip de Ste. Croix

ISBN 978-1-4454-2003-5

Printed in China

Page 1: *The circular ring of large standing stones at Stonehenge in Wiltshire, UK is one of the most famous Neolithic sites in the world. It is believed that the iconic stone monument was erected around 2500 BC.*

Page 2: *The Great Wall of China – one of the world's finest feats of building – was constructed over many centuries.*

Page 3: *Monument Valley on the southern border of Utah with northern Arizona, USA, is a region of the Colorado Plateau characterized by a cluster of vast and iconic sandstone buttes, the largest reaching 300m (1000ft) above the valley floor.*

Right: *America's Grand Canyon, a steep-sided gorge carved by the Colorado River in Arizona, stretches an awesome 446km (277 miles) in length, ranges in width from 6.4 to 29km (4 to 18 miles) and attains a depth of over 1.83km (6000 feet).*

Contents

Introduction

It is all too easy in this fast-paced age to become indifferent to the extraordinary beauty – both natural and man-made – that surrounds us in every corner of the Earth. But, as this spectacular book reveals, if we can stand back sufficiently and try to see the world afresh, remarkable sights lie all around.

The first section is entitled Natural Wonders. Here we are taken on a fantastic journey to some of the most awe-inspiring places on Earth. We witness the very forces that shaped the landscape and geology of our planet still at work as they manifest themselves in the form of canyons and gorges gouged out of the land, thundering waterfalls, towering rock formations, exotic reef systems, placid, mysterious lakes, spouting geysers, extraordinary mountains, glacial rivers of ice, and the bringers of fire from within the Earth itself – volcanoes.

Next we turn to the incredible monuments that still stand as evidence of the greatest of the world's ancient civilizations – pyramids, temples, mausoleums, fortifications, effigies, memorials to great leaders, even places of sacrifice – all these astonishing engineering achievements bear witness to the enduring capacity of humankind to raise great buildings as a concrete expression of cultural identity. The roll call encompasses ancient Egypt, Greece and Rome, the Minoan and Persian civilizations, China, the Mayan, Aztec and Inca remains from Central and South America, and Burmese and Khmer masterpieces from Asia.

The final section, Sacred Stone, unites the natural world with the crafted works of humankind concentrating as it does on the stone-built monuments that have inhabited the landscape from Neolithic times to the relatively recent past. These include mighty stone burial chambers, rings of standing stones (or henges), temples and churches literally hewn from the rock, the moai stone heads of Easter Island, and sites where petroglyphs – rock paintings and carvings – reveal the ancient religious and ceremonial longings of our early forefathers.

Right: Most archaeologists believe that the ancient Peruvian city of Machu Picchu was built as an estate for the Inca emperor Pachacuti (1438–1472). Often referred to as 'The Lost City of the Incas', it is perhaps the most familiar and spectacular icon of the Inca world.

Natural Wonders

Right and below: The Grand Canyon is a steep-sided gorge carved out by the Colorado River as it flows through the US state of Arizona. It is largely contained within the Grand Canyon National Park, one of the first national parks to be established in the USA. Living up to its name, the Grand Canyon is 446km (277 miles) long, ranges in width from 6.4 to 29km (4 to 18 miles) and is over a mile (1.83km) deep.

Opposite: The Grand Canyon is renowned for its remarkable size and its spectacular colours. Geologically it is significant because of the sequence of ancient rocks that are beautifully preserved and exposed in the walls of the canyon. These rock layers record much of the early geological history of the North American continent.

Below: The spectacular and beautiful Havasu Falls, on the Havasupai Indian Reservation, are located in a remote canyon within Grand Canyon National Park. The twin plumes plunge some 30m (100ft) over cliffs into a turquoise pool.

Opposite and left: Bryce Canyon in southwestern Utah, USA, is a giant natural amphitheatre created by erosion, which sculpted its distinctive rock spires called hoodoos.

Right: Tiger Leaping Gorge, a canyon on the Yangtze River in China, is one of the world's deepest river canyons with steep cliffs towering 2km (1.25 miles) above the waters.

Below: The Verdon Gorge in Provence, southern France, is famed for the blue-green colour of its river. It is about 25km (15.5 miles) in length and up to 700m (2300ft) deep.

Right: The mighty Victoria Falls on the Zambezi River in southern Africa are situated on the border between Zambia and Zimbabwe. The falls, some of the largest in the world, are formed as the river plummets in a single vertical drop. They were named by the explorer David Livingstone.

Below: The Niagara Falls, on the Niagara River, straddle the border between the Canadian province of Ontario and the US state of New York. The falls are composed of two major sections: Horseshoe Falls (pictured) which lies mainly in Canada and American Falls on the US side of the border.

Opposite: The Iguaçu Falls are located on the border of Brazil and Argentina and consist of a system of 275 waterfalls along a 2.7km (1.67 mile) stretch of the Iguaçu River. The huge curtains of water are among the most visually dramatic of all the world's waterfalls.

Below: Angel Falls is the world's highest waterfall. It is 979m (3212ft) high and plunges 807m (2647ft) from the edge of the Auyantepui mountain in the Canaima National Park, Venezuela. It was named after Jimmie Angel, a US aviator who was the first to fly over the falls in 1933.

Far left: The Wave is a colourful, undulating sandstone rock formation located near the border between the US states of Arizona and Utah, on the slopes of the Coyote Buttes.

Left: Delicate Arch, a 16m (52ft) high, free-standing natural sandstone arch, is the best-known landmark in Arches National Park near Moab, Utah, USA.

Below: Familiar from many Wild West movies, the iconic West Mitten Butte, East Mitten Butte and Merrick Butte formations in Monument Valley, Arizona, USA.

Left: Uluru, also known as Ayers Rock, is a large sandstone formation in the southern part of the Northern Territory, central Australia. Lying 335km (208 miles) southwest of the nearest large town, Alice Springs, it is one of Australia's most famous landmarks. It stands 348m (1142ft) high and measures 9.4km (5.8 miles) around the base. Most of its vast bulk is hidden below the ground. Sacred to the Aboriginal people of the area, Uluru appears to change colour as light strikes it at different times of the day and the year. Sunset often provides a particularly remarkable sight when the rock briefly glows red in the darkening landscape.

Above: Brooding karst limestone peaks dominate the landscape along the Li river near Yangshuo, Guanxi province, China. The distinctive rock formations typical of a karst landscape are caused by the erosion of parts of the limestone bedrock as a result of the action of water.

Left: The three imposing granite monoliths of Torres del Paine are the best-known and most spectacular summits in the Cordillera del Paine group of mountains in Chile's Torres del Paine National Park. Shaped by the forces of glacial ice, the peaks overlook a small lake set high in the mountains.

Left and below: The Great Barrier Reef is a true wonder of the world – it is the largest structure created by living organisms. Located off the coast of Queensland in the northeastern area of Australia, this beautiful reef system is composed of tiny coral polyps. It is made up of approximately 900 islands and 3000 separate coral reefs.

Right: The Great Barrier Reef is home to a dazzling variety of marine life. Studies have revealed an amazing number of species, including 125 varieties of sharks and stingrays, 49 species of pipefish and around 1500 types of fish.

Left: A deserted tropical coral island in Okinawa Prefecture, Japan. Warm ocean currents here create ideal conditions for many marine species and some of the world's finest coral reefs.

Below: The Maldives, formed by numerous natural atolls and reefs, boast crystalline lagoons studded with multi-coloured corals and warm, azure seas teeming with exotic marine life.

Bottom: The coral reef is one of the most diverse ecosystems on our planet. Around 25 per cent of the world's marine species are found in and around reef systems.

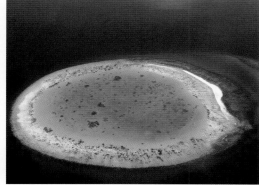

Above: Wizard Island in Crater Lake, a caldera lake in the US state of Oregon. Famed for its deep blue colour, it measures 8 by 10km (5 by 6 miles). Average depth is 350m (1150ft).

Right: Heaven Lake is a crater lake on the border between China and North Korea, lying high atop the volcanic Baekdu Mountain. A large lake monster is rumoured to live here.

Far right: The stunning colour of Bolivia's salt lake, Laguna Verde, is caused by deposits containing copper and other minerals. Licancábur volcano towers in the distance.

Left: At more than 25 million years old, Lake Baikal in Siberia is the world's oldest lake. It is the most voluminous freshwater lake in the world with an average depth of 745m (2442ft) and it contains almost 20 per cent of the world's surface fresh water.

Below: The Dead Sea is a salt lake (one of the world's saltiest) bordering Israel and Jordan. Its surface is 422m (1385ft) below sea level, the lowest elevation on the Earth's surface on land. Its level is falling because water from the River Jordan is being diverted for irrigation purposes.

Above: White Dome geyser is a large cone-type geyser located in the Lower Geyser Basin in Yellowstone National Park, Wyoming, USA. Its eruptions are unpredictable, with intervals ranging from 15 minutes to three hours, and they may last between two to three minutes at a time.

Above right: Castle geyser in the Upper Geyser Basin of Yellowstone National Park is noted for the deposits which form its cone which looks like a castle turret. It has a 10–12-hour eruption cycle and blasts out hot water for about 20 minutes in a vertical column that reaches 27m (90ft) in height.

Right: Old Faithful is probably the best known geyser in Yellowstone National Park. It was named in 1870, the first geyser in the park to achieve this distinction. Eruptions can shoot 14,000 to 32,000 litres (3080 to 7000 gallons) of boiling water and steam to a height of 30–56m (106–185ft) and can last anything from 90 seconds to five minutes. The average height of an eruption is 44m (145ft) but the highest recorded spout measured 56m (185ft) in height. Intervals between eruptions can range from 45 minutes to a little over two hours. Over the years the average length of the interval has slowly increased, which may be the result of earthquake activity.

Left: *Strokkur is a geyser in the geothermic region beside the Hvítá River in the southwest of Iceland, east of Reykjavik. It is one of Iceland's most famous and reliable geysers, erupting regularly to a height of around 16m (52ft) every four to eight minutes. Strokkur is Icelandic for 'churn'.*

Below: *This spectacular geyser, known as Pohutu (meaning 'big splash'), is found in the Whakarewarewa Thermal Valley near Rotorua, New Zealand. It erupts two or three times per hour, bubbling up from below the ground and shooting a plume of hot water and steam up to 30m (100ft) high.*

Right: Mount Kilimanjaro in northeastern Tanzania, Africa, is among the tallest free-standing mountains in the world, rising 4600m (15,100ft) from its base. It is a giant stratovolcano that began to form around a million years ago. Two of its three peaks, Mawenzi and Shira, are extinct while Kibo (the highest peak) is dormant and so could erupt again.

Below: Mount Fuji is the highest mountain in Japan at 3776m (12,388ft) and is an active stratovolcano. Its symmetrical cone is an icon of Japan and it is frequently depicted in art, such as in the prints by Katsushika Hokusai.

Above: The defining feature of Table Mountain in South Africa is a level plateau measuring about 3km (2 miles) across, surrounded by steep cliffs. The plateau, flanked by Devil's Peak to the east and by Lion's Head to the west, forms a dramatic backdrop to Cape Town and Table Bay harbour.

Opposite: The Matterhorn, on the border between Switzerland and Italy, soars to a height of 4478m (14,692ft), making it one of the highest peaks in the Alps. The first ascent was made in 1865 by an expedition led by Edward Whymper and ended tragically when most of the climbers fell to their deaths on the descent.

Above: A dramatic panorama of a glacier on Spitsbergen Island, Svalbard, Norway. A significant number of glaciers in Svalbard are surging-type glaciers, which means that from time to time they advance very quickly, relatively speaking, moving up to several miles during just four or five years.

Left: Jostedalsbreen is a large plateau glacier with numerous branches and is the biggest glacier in continental Europe. It is found on the west coast of southern Norway. This great river of ice is more than 60km (37 miles) long, is 600m (1970ft) deep at its thickest point and covers an area of some 480km^2 (185sq miles).

Right: A bridge of ice in Perito Moreno glacier in Los Glaciares National Park, Patagonia, Argentina. This 250km^2 (97sq mile) ice formation measures 30km (19 miles) in length and is famous for its blue coloration caused by trapped oxygen molecules. The glacier flows out into the waters of Lago Argentino.

Opposite: Glacier Bay National Park and Preserve in southeastern Alaska. Glaciers descending from the snow-capped mountains into the bay create spectacular displays. The glaciers are currently retreating which allows scientists to observe what happens as new life colonizes the bare soil.

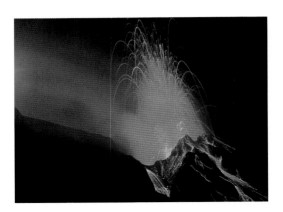

Left: Mount Etna, an active stratovolcano on the east coast of Sicily, is the largest active volcano in Europe. It is currently 3329m (10,922ft) high, though this varies with summit eruptions.

Right: Stromboli, a small volcanic island north of Sicily, has been erupting almost continuously for at least the last 20,000 years. It is nicknamed the 'lighthouse of the Mediterranean'.

Below: Mount Bromo, an active volcano in East Java, Indonesia, rises to a height of 2329m (7641ft) in the middle of a vast plain called the Sand Sea – a protected nature reserve.

Left and below: *Hawaii Volcanoes National Park, established in 1916, is located on the Pacific island of Hawaii and includes Kilauea, one of the world's most active volcanoes, and Mauna Loa, which is at 4169m (13,677ft) the world's most massive volcano. Eruptions here are not particularly violent, and the most common form involves lava fountains feeding lava flows. Typically, at the start of an eruption, a rift up to several miles long opens, with lava fountains occurring along its length in a so-called 'curtain of fire'.*

Civilizations

Ancient Egypt

Below: The Great Sphinx of Giza is a statue of a reclining lion with a human head that stands on the Giza plateau in Giza close to the Great Pyramid, near modern-day Cairo in Egypt. It is the largest monolith statue in the world and was sculpted from a limestone outcrop. Standing 73.5m (241ft) long, 6m (20ft) wide and 20m (66ft) high, it is believed to have been built by ancient Egyptians between 2555 BC and 2532 BC. The face portrayed is that of the royal king Khafre.

Left: The Karnak Temple complex near Luxor, some 500km (300 miles) south of Cairo in Egypt, comprises a vast assortment of ruined temples, obelisks and sacred buildings. It is the largest temple complex ever built, and represents the combined achievement of many generations of ancient builders. Construction of temples started in the Middle Kingdom around 2040 BC and continued through to Ptolemaic times in around the 4th century BC. Approximately 30 pharaohs contributed to the programme of building. Few of the individual features of Karnak are unique, but the sheer size and number of features are overwhelming.

Below: The Great Pyramid of Giza is the oldest and largest of the three pyramids in the Giza necropolis bordering what is now El Giza, Egypt. It is the oldest of the Seven Wonders of the Ancient World and the only one that survives substantially intact. It is believed that the pyramid was built as a tomb for fourth dynasty Egyptian pharaoh Khufu and was constructed over a 20-year period concluding around 2550 BC. Originally the Great Pyramid was covered by a layer of casing stones that formed a smooth outer surface. The sides were angled at 52° so that symbolically the pyramids represented solar rays in honour of the Sun god Ra.

Left: These statues are in the courtyard of the Rameses III temple at Karnak. Rameses III reigned from 1187 to 1156 BC. During his 31-year reign, Rameses built the vast mortuary complex at Medinet Habu and three shrines at Karnak that were dedicated to the gods Amun, Mut and Khonsu.

Below: Columns, pylons and obelisks at Karnak frequently bear hieroglyphic inscriptions like these. Such characters were originally pictograms and were named hieroglyphs (Greek for sacred writing) because of their use in religious contexts. In ancient Egypt they were written from right to left.

Minoan Civilization

This page: Knossos is the largest Bronze Age site on the island of Crete and was probably the ceremonial and political centre of the Minoan civilization which flourished on Crete between c.3000–1400 BC. The palace was a maze of workrooms, living spaces and store rooms set around a central square and may have housed around 40,000 people.

Opposite: Part of the Minoan palace at Knossos, reconstructed by British archaeologist Sir Arthur Evans who excavated and, somewhat controversially, restored the site in 1900.

Persian Empire

These pages: *Persepolis was the ceremonial capital of the Persian Empire during the Achaemenid dynasty (c.550–330 BC). The magnificent palace complex at Persepolis was founded by Darius the Great around 518 BC, although more than a century passed before it was finally completed. Many of the walls were decorated with intricate bas relief sculptures depicting scenes of soldiers, nobles and animals. The wealth of the empire was evident in all aspects of its construction but its splendour was relatively short-lived as the palaces were looted and burned by Alexander the Great in 331–330 BC.*

Ancient China

Right and below: The Terracotta Army was discovered in 1974 in the eastern suburbs of Xi'an, Shaanxi Province, China, by local farmers drilling a water well. The Terracotta Army consists of more than 7500 life-size terracotta warriors (each with a differently modelled face) and their weapons, chariots and war horses. They were buried to guard the tomb of Qin Shih Huangdi (ruled 246–221 BC), the First Emperor of the Qin Dynasty. It is estimated that it took around 700,000 labourers to build the vast mausoleum, with its interior representing a miniature empire, and the man-made mountain above it.

Opposite: The Great Wall of China is a series of stone and earthen fortifications in northern China, built originally to protect the northern borders of the Chinese Empire against intrusions by various nomadic groups including the Mongols from the north. The Wall was begun in 221 BC and has been rebuilt and maintained many times between the 5th century BC and the final 16th-century Ming Dynasty construction. The Great Wall stretches along an arc from Shanhaiguan in the east to Lop Nur in the west and recent surveys estimate that the entire Great Wall, including all of its branches, measures 8850km (5500 miles) in length.

Ancient Greece

Right and below right: The Parthenon, which sits atop the Acropolis in Athens, is a temple dedicated to the Greek goddess Athena, and is one of the world's greatest cultural monuments. The Parthenon was built between 447 and 438 BC and replaced an older temple of Athena that was destroyed in the Persian invasion of 480 BC.

Below: A detail of the Porch of the Caryatids, a structure which forms part of the Erechtheum – an ancient Greek temple on the north side of Athens' Acropolis.

Below: Delphi is an important archaeological site in Greece, located on the southwestern spur of Mount Parnassus in the valley of Phocis. In Greek mythology, Delphi was the site of the Delphic oracle, the most important oracle in the classical Greek world, and was a major site for the worship of the god Apollo. Enquirers would, upon payment of a fee, put their questions to Apollo's medium, a priestess called the Pythia. The Tholos at the sanctuary of Athena Pronaia (pictured) is a circular building that was constructed between 380 and 360 BC. It consisted of 20 Doric columns arranged in a circle, with ten Corinthian columns forming an inner circle.

Top: The most notable ruin of ancient Corinth is the 6th-century BC Temple of Apollo. The temple was built around 560 BC, while the majority of other temples to Apollo were built a century later. It was destroyed by earthquakes but seven of the original 38 Doric columns still stand.

Above: Olympia, an ancient Greek sanctuary in Elis, was the site of the Olympic Games in classical times. The Philippeion (pictured) at Olympia was an Ionic circular memorial of ivory and gold built in celebration of Philip II of Macedon's victory at the battle of Chaeronea (338 BC).

Ancient Rome

Below: The Colosseum in Rome, Italy, is an ancient amphitheatre in the centre of the city, the largest ever built in the Roman Empire. It is considered one of the greatest works of Roman architecture and engineering. Its construction began between AD 70 and 72 under the Emperor Vespasian and was completed in AD 80 under Titus. Capable of seating 50,000 spectators, the Colosseum was used for gladiatorial contests and games as well as public spectacles. Its opening by Emperor Titus was marked by 100 days of games during which around 9000 animals and hundreds of gladiators died.

Top: Leptis Magna was an important city of the Roman Empire and its ruins are located on the coast at Al Khums, Libya. The theatre (pictured) was built during the reign of Emperor Augustus in AD 1–2 and subsequently renovated by Caracalla. It is among the largest of the entire Roman world.

Above: Sabratha, in Libya, was absorbed into the Roman Empire in 146 BC after the fall of the Punic Empire. The amphitheatre here was built between AD 175 and 200, and is the most complete theatre surviving from the Roman world. It has 25 entrances and could accommodate an audience of 5000 people.

Left: The elegant Pont du Gard aqueduct in the south of France was the work of Roman engineers. It was long thought to have been built by Augustus' son-in-law and aide, Marcus Vipsanius Agrippa, around the year 19 BC. Newer excavations, however, suggest the construction may have taken place in the middle of the 1st century AD. The aqueduct's stones – some of which weigh up to 6 tonnes – were precisely cut to fit perfectly together, eliminating the need for mortar. The masonry was lifted into place by block and tackle with a massive human-powered treadmill providing the power for the winch. The aqueduct delivered 20,000m³ (4.4 million gallons) of water daily.

Above: The Temple of Hadrian in Ephesus, Turkey, features a beautiful arch as part of the front facade and reliefs of Medusa and other mythological scenes inside. It was erected around AD 118 by Publius Quintilius and was dedicated not only to Emperor Hadrian but also to the goddess Artemis.

Left: The Library of Celsus is one of the most beautiful Roman structures in Ephesus. It was built in AD 117 and was a monumental tomb for Gaius Julius Celsus Polemaeanus, the governor of the province of Asia. It contained more than 12,000 manuscript scrolls kept in special wall niches.

Mayan Civilization

Above: Yaxchilan is an ancient Mayan city located on the bank of the Usumacinta River in what is now the state of Chiapas, Mexico. It flourished during the Late Classic Period around AD 600–900. The site is famous for its sculptured stone lintels containing hieroglyphic texts.

Below: The ancient Mayan city of Palenque lies in the jungles of Chiapas, Mexico. Palenque is a medium-sized archaeological site, much smaller than such sites as Tikal or Copán, but it contains some of the finest architecture, sculpture and bas-relief carvings that the Maya ever produced.

Above: The Pyramid of the Magician at Uxmal, a large pre-Columbian Mayan city in the state of Yucatán, Mexico. It stands around 35m (115ft) tall. The Uxmal area was occupied as early as 800 BC, but the major building period took place when it was the capital of a Late Classic Mayan state around AD 850–925.

Right: Tikal in northern Guatemala is one of the largest sites of the pre-Columbian Mayan civilization. Tikal Temple I which measures 47m (154ft) in height is also known as the Temple of the Great Jaguar because it features a carved lintel that represents a king sitting upon a jaguar throne.

Above: The Mayan Pyramid of Kukulkan 'El Castillo' as seen from the Platform of the Eagles and the Jaguars, Chichén Itzá, Mexico. At the spring and autumn equinox, as the sun rises and sets, the corner of the structure casts a shadow in the shape of a plumed serpent – the Mesoamerican god Kukulkan or Quetzalcoatl – along the north staircase.

Left: The main temple structure in the ancient Mayan city at Tulum overlooks the Gulf of Mexico. Tulum was protected on the seaward side by steep cliffs and on the landward side by a thick wall that averaged about 5m (16ft) in height.

Burmese Empire

These pages: Bagan in Burma (Myanmar) was the ancient capital of several Burmese kingdoms. It is located on the banks of the Irrawaddy River, 140km (90 miles) southwest of Mandalay. Bagan may have been settled as far back as the 2nd century AD, but by the mid-9th century it had become established as the capital of the Burmese empire. Most of the 2200 structures that still survive at Bagan are temples and stupas – Buddhist mound-like structures which are believed to contain relics or remains of individuals. Some stupas are reputed to contain remains of Buddhist holy men or even of the Guatama Buddha himself.

Angkorian Empire

Below: Angkor Wat is a huge temple complex at Angkor, near Siem Reap, Cambodia. It was built for the king Suryavarman II in the early 12th century. The moated temple area represented the universe with the pyramidal shrine at the centre symbolizing the sacred Himalayan peak of Mount Meru.

Right and far right: Angkor Wat, the largest religious edifice in the world, is set amidst the Cambodian jungle. Enormous tree roots have grown to envelop some of the abandoned remains of the ancient Khmer temples.

Above and right: Dating from the 12th century, Bayon Temple is the central temple of the ancient city of Angkor Thom, located just to the north of Angkor Wat. Bayon is famous for its huge stone faces, with one facing outward and keeping watch at each compass point.

Left: About 20km (12 miles) north of Angkor, Banteay Srei is a 10th-century Khmer temple dedicated to the Hindu god Shiva. It is built of red sandstone, which lends itself to the elaborate wall carvings which are still well preserved today. The buildings themselves are unusually small in scale.

Aztec and Incan Civilizations

Opposite: The Incan city of Machu Picchu nestles 2430m (8000ft) above sea level in an extraordinarily beautiful setting on the eastern slopes of the Andes in Peru. It is often referred to as 'The Lost City of the Incas' as it was never found by the 16th-century Spanish conquistadors.

Below: Teotihuacan in the Basin of Mexico contains some of the largest pyramidal structures built in the pre-Columbian Americas. The city reached its peak in AD 450, when it was the centre of a powerful culture throughout much of Mesoamerica.

Left: El Tajín, north of the port of Veracruz in Mexico, was the site of one of the largest and most important cities of the Classic Era of Mesoamerica. The city flourished from AD 600 to 1200 and during this time numerous temples, pyramids, palaces and courts for ball games were built here.

Below: This Inca site at Moray in Peru's Sacred Valley a little northwest of Cusco is believed to have been a 'laboratory' to allow Inca farmers to study the effect of altitude and varying weather conditions on different plants and crop types. The concentric terraces are up to 150m (500ft) deep.

Sacred Stone

Below: Poulnabrone Dolmen is a portal tomb in the Burren, County Clare, Ireland, dating back to the Neolithic period, probably constructed between 4200 BC to 2900 BC. The dolmen consists of a 3.6m- (12ft-) long, slab-like, tabular capstone supported by two slender portal stones, which lift the capstone 1.8m (6ft) from the ground. The people who were buried in Poulnabrone dolmen were Neolithic farmers. The name literally means 'the hole of the sorrows'.

Above: Megalithic temples at Hagar Qim in Malta dating from 3600–3200 BC. Malta's megalithic temples are amongst the most ancient religious sites on Earth. Bones of numerous sacrificial animals have been found here as well as many statuettes of deities and highly decorated pottery.

Below: At 40m (130ft) high, Silbury Hill – an artificial chalk mound near Avebury, Wiltshire, UK – is the tallest prehistoric human-made mound in Europe and one of the largest in the world. It was built around 2500 BC and would have taken years to construct. Its exact purpose is unknown.

Left: *Megalithic tombs and dolmens are found in Europe from the Baltic south to Spain and Portugal (pictured). A dolmen is a type of single-chamber tomb, usually consisting of three or more upright stones supporting a large capstone. They were usually covered with earth to form a barrow.*

Below: *Carreg Samson is a 3000-year-old Neolithic burial chamber on the Pembroke coast, Wales. The capstone, measuring 4.5m (15ft) long by 2.8m (9ft) wide is supported on three of the seven upright stones, and the whole structure was once covered by a mound of earth or stones.*

Far left: *The large Sa Coveccada dolmen in Sardinia, Italy, stands an impressive 2.7m (8.8ft) tall and 5m (16ft) long, with a capstone measuring 6m (20ft) long by 3m (10ft) wide by 60cm (2ft) deep and weighing in at 27 tonnes.*

Left: *Li Lolghi is Sardinia's largest giant's tomb – the name given by local people and archaeologists to a type of Sardinian megalithic gallery grave. These monuments were constructed all over the island – mainly by the Bronze Age nuraghi builders – from about 1900 BC until the invasion by Carthaginian forces, almost 1000 years later.*

Opposite: Stonehenge in Wiltshire is one of the most famous prehistoric monuments in the world – its earliest phases date back to 3000 BC. It is composed of a circular setting of large standing stones and is at the centre of the most dense complex of Neolithic and Bronze Age monuments in England.

Below: The Callanish standing stone circle is an ancient site on the Isle of Lewis, in the Outer Hebrides, Scotland. This cross-shaped setting of standing stones, with 13 primary stones forming an inner circle, was erected around 2000 BC and is one of the most spectacular megalithic monuments in Scotland.

Left: Smooth-sided sandstone pillars of the impressive Bronze Age Drombeg circle perch on a rocky terrace in County Cork, Ireland. A high portal stone rises opposite a long recumbent – the midpoint of which has a notch set in line with distant hills to provide a sightline to the winter solstice sunset.

Below: Avebury in Wiltshire is the site of a large henge (prehistoric circular monument) and is one of the largest Neolithic sites in Europe. Within the henge is a great stone circle with a diameter of 335m (1099ft) which originally comprised 98 standing stones, some weighing 40 tonnes or more.

Left and above: The sandstone blocks in Kakadu National Park, Northern Territory, Australia, contain one of the greatest concentrations of Aboriginal rock art in the world. Approximately 5000 art sites have been recorded featuring rich ochre paintings, some of which may date back 50,000 years.

Below: Cueva de las Manos (Spanish for Cave of the Hands) in Patagonia, Argentina, is decorated with 9000-year-old stencilled images of human hands that were created by spraying mineral-based paint onto the cave walls through bone pipes. Hunting scenes and animals are also pictured.

Left: Caves in the Drakensberg Mountains, South Africa, are richly decorated with between 35,000 and 40,000 works of art made by indigenous bushmen. This is the largest collection of such work in the world. These paintings are difficult to date, but there is evidence that the bushman civilization existed in the Drakensberg at least 40,000 years ago.

Below: The sandstone rocks at Twyfelfontein in northwestern Namibia are covered with around 2000 carvings created by bushmen that depict rhinoceroses, elephants, ostriches and giraffes, as well as human and animal footprints.

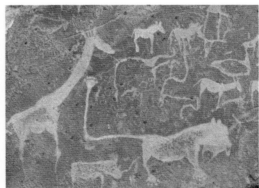

Left: Newspaper Rock State Historic Monument in eastern Utah, USA, features an 18.5m² (200sq ft) flat rock covered with one of the largest known collections of petroglyphs. Depicting humans, animals and abstract forms, they were carved by Native Americans around 2000 years ago.

Right: The rock carvings at Alta are part of an ancient site near the town of Alta in northern Norway. More than 5000 petroglyphs have been found on several sites in the area with the earliest dating to around 4200 BC. The imagery reveals a culture of hunter-gatherers who pursued animals and fish.

These pages: *Petra in Jordan is a unique city carved into the sandstone rockface by the Nabataeans, an ancient Semitic people who settled here more than 2000 years ago, turning it into an important junction on the silk, spice and commercial trade routes. Entrance to the city is through the Siq, a narrow gorge flanked on either side by dazzlingly coloured cliffs. At the end of the Siq is the Al-Khazneh (Treasury, seen left), with its awe-inspiring and massive facade, 30m (100ft) wide and 43m (140ft) high, carved out of the rockface and dwarfing everything around it. In the surrounding Petra valley there are hundreds o elaborate rock-cut temples and tombs with intricate carvings.*

These pages: Moai is the Polynesian name given to the monolithic human figures carved from volcanic tufa rock on Easter Island, Chile, between AD 1250 and 1500. Most of them have overly large heads three-fifths the size of their bodies, with long noses and broad chins. It is thought that they either represented ancient gods or the faces of ancestral tribal leaders. When they were first erected, the recessed eye sockets would have contained white coral eyes with black or red pupils. Some moai would also have borne pukao topknots carved out of red scoria rock. These might have represented the feather headdresses of Polynesian chieftains.

Opposite: Mesa Verde National Park in Colorado, USA, preserves a spectacular reminder of ancient Puebloan culture created by a people called the Anasazi who flourished here from AD 550 to 1300. The park contains over 4000 archaeological sites including cliff dwellings and pithouses, pueblos, masonry towers and farming structures. Cliff Palace (pictured) is the largest cliff dwelling at Mesa Verde. It has 150 rooms, plus an additional 75 open areas. Twenty-one of the rooms are kivas (underground or partly underground chambers) and 25 to 30 rooms appear to be residential. It is estimated that 100 to 120 Anasazi lived in Cliff Palace at any one time.

Above: Canyon de Chelly National Monument in northeastern Arizona, USA, preserves ruins of the early indigenous tribes that lived in the area, including the Anasazi and Navajo. White House Ruin (pictured) is the largest and most spectacular of the many ruins in the canyon area.

Left: Between AD 900 and 1150, Chaco Canyon in New Mexico, USA, was a major centre of culture for the ancient Puebloans. They quarried sandstone blocks and hauled timber from great distances, assembling 15 major complexes. Shown here are the remains of a kiva used for religious rituals.

Left: The Leshan Giant Buddha in Sichuan province, China, was built between AD 713 and 803 during the Tang Dynasty. The 71m (213ft) tall stone sculpture is carved out of a cliff face and is the largest carved stone Buddha in the world. At the time of its construction, it was the tallest statue in the world.

Below: The entrance and elephant statue in the Jain Temple at Ellora Caves, near Aurangabad, India. Between AD 600 and 1000 Buddhist, Hindu and Jain monks carved chapels, temples and monasteries from an escarpment and decorated them with sculptures of remarkable imagination and detail.

Far left and left: The Ajanta Caves in Maharashtra, India, comprise 29 cave monuments excavated out of the granite rock of a long cliff face. They were created between the 1st century BC and 5th century AD and contain paintings and sculptures considered to be masterpieces of Buddhist religious pictorial art. The caves were built as secluded retreats for Buddhist monks. Using only simple tools like a hammer and chisel, the monks carved out the multitude of impressive figures adorning the stone walls of these structures. Fresco paintings depict colourful Buddhist legends and divinities with a vitality that is unsurpassed in Indian art.

Left and above: Borobudur is a 9th-century Buddhist temple in Magelang, Central Java, Indonesia. Borobudur stupa is the world's largest Buddhist monument. It comprises six square platforms topped by three circular platforms, and is decorated with 2672 relief panels and 504 Buddha statues. A main dome, located at the centre of the top platform, is surrounded by 72 Buddha statues seated inside a perforated stupa. Approximately 55,000m^3 (1,942,000ft^3) of stones were cut to size and transported from neighbouring rivers and laid without mortar to build the monument. It lay abandoned for 800 years before it was rediscovered in the 19th century.

Left and below: The Church of Saint George is the most finely executed and best preserved of 11 medieval churches excavated in the 13th century out of the rocky hills of Lalibela, a town in northern Ethiopia, Africa. The roofs of the Lalibela churches are level with the ground and they are reached by stairs descending into narrow trenches. The churches are connected by tunnels and walkways and stretch across sheer drops. The Church of Saint George measures 25m (82ft) square by 30m (100ft) high. Its roof forms the shape of a Greek cross. There is a small baptismal pool outside the church, which stands in a man-made trench.

This page: Göreme is a town in Cappadocia, an historical region of Turkey set among a landscape of 'fairy chimney' rock formations – tall spires of rock formed from volcanic ash and lava that resulted from the eruption of Mount Erciyes about 2000 years ago. In this spectacular setting, entirely sculpted by erosion, the Göreme valley and its surroundings contain a multitude of rock-hewn dwellings, sanctuaries and churches, which date back to the 4th century. These Christian edifices contain many unique examples of Byzantine art. During the 7th century new churches were dug into the rocks and these were richly decorated with colourful frescoes.

Index